Life, Love and Wonder

Carolyne T Aneh

BookLeaf
Publishing

India | USA | UK

Presentation by *BookLeaf Publishing*

Web: www.bookleafpub.com

E-mail: info@bookleafpub.com

ISBN: 9789358317886

First edition 2024

*My family and friends, whose support,
especially over the recent years, has added
an immeasurable amount to my personal
growth.*

PREFACE

Life is full of ups and downs and everything else in between. I hope you get to hear my heart on these scribbles. The purpose of this short book was to share my experiences and how disorganised Life can be. Often found jumping from one emotion to the next, with no warning.

Granted, not everything in here will be factual, I don't intend it to be. However, all of these poems are born from my unlimited exposure to the enchantment that is known as Life.

Maybe, you might read a piece that resonates with you, and you feel as though our thoughts are aligned. Or maybe you might be swayed to see something from a different angle altogether. Perhaps it might be both. Either way, I just hope that you encounter something familiar. After all, other people have walked the path of life way before we ever came to be.

Beginning

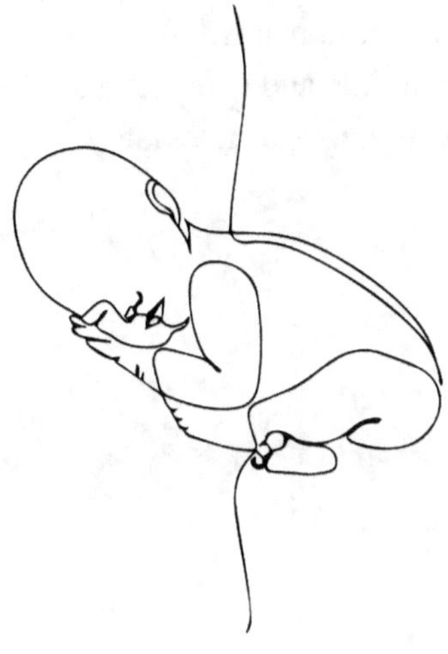

I begin.
From a place where my consciousness
Had not been given permission to exist. Yet.
I am nowhere.
I am nothing.
Waiting for the moment
I can be permitted to fully form.
Waiting in the darkness.
Growing,
Waiting,
Growing,
Until I have passed the gift of patience.

I open my eyes to the world of senseless wonder,
Incomprehensible, yet content.

Lacking awareness of anything,
Sitting there bundled,
Handled, by warm hands.
That through time and many an age,
I would get to know, as my clan.

Life

As the ink runs through my pen,
My heart is activated in allowing my mind
To explore the corners where men seldom reach,
I pause and reflect on Life.

Life, does it know me? Can it grasp who I am?
Can I stretch out my hands and let it hold me
and support my stance?
Can it show me everything in clear light, leaving
no room for qualms or doubt?
Life, Am I living it right?

Life, where is the knowledge it imparts?
Knowledge of how to cry, how to rebuild the
broken pieces of my soul?

How to render still anxieties of the unknown,
Life, can it say I have grown?

Can it show me the way,
to the place where I can be free?
A place where I can be me? Where I do not need
to pretend.
Can it show me how to not continue wearing the
masks of missed chances,
Life, can it give me a cheat code, show me the
best stances?

Caution

Even if you were
A little teddy bear
You would not have my heart
No matter how fuzzy you were

For looks can be deceiving
And nothing seen can be trusted
In fact not everything that you hear
Is worth believing

No Guarantees

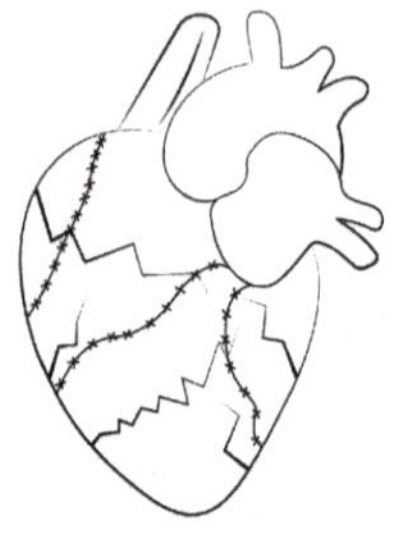

Life ain't that bad.
It's the people in it that are strange.
Human behaviour remains a mystery.

Ever experienced breaking your heart,
To the point where,
It cost you an extra charge to fix it?

So you decide to gather the pieces,
Put them in a jar and just look at them.

I want help, but I don't know how to accept it.
I don't think I ever will.
Because once you ask for help
That's a queue for rest of the world
To start peering through your life.

The only guarantee in life

Is—there's no guarantee at all.
We are all here surviving on hope,
Or faith, or maybe both.
Or maybe, we're all just living in free fall.

Maintaining The Balance

Compromise can come easy or hard
Like a wrong corrected by another.
Left and right, up and down
Untouched regardless of pressure.

Darkness restricted by lightness,
The same way 'bad' follows 'good.'
The balance between the two,
Remains flawless and understood.

Whether standing or sitting,
Or silent or singing,
The gap cannot be changed.
Perspectives may differ,
And opinions may wither,
You're either a winner or a loser.

Compromise aims to do no harm,
But handle it with endless care.
Although it CAN have a 'positive' outcome,
Sitting opposite is a 'negative' dare.

The balance should be maintained,
Like a conversation between two souls.
Who hardly use words to communicate.
They rarely speak; for mostly, they listen.

Safe Delivery

Please don't drop the coffin,
There's a body in there, you know.
It never ceases to amaze me;
How nature carries its flow.

Please don't drop the coffin,
You have to pay respect, you know.
Although they're now in our absence;
We will soon follow where they go.

Please don't drop the coffin,
It's a scary thought, you know.
For the living know that they will die;
Yet there's a lot, the dead don't know.

Please don't drop the coffin,
They need to stay intact, you know.
'cause when the Body meets the ground;
Their bones the wind shouldn't blow.

Please don't drop the coffin,
There's a Body in there, you know.
It will never cease to amaze me;
How nature carries its flow.

The Waiting Game

How long must I wait?
Before I have waited long enough,
For time is endless, it will never stop moving
So how long must I wait?

How long must I wait?
It seems like time is standing still.
As a matter of fact, it's ticking backwards
So how long must I wait?

How long must I wait?
Frustrated tension is rising,
And ingratitude is a nasty sin
So how long must I wait?

How long must I wait?
I've been betrayed by my kindness
Betrayed by my inexperienced trust,
So how long must I wait?

Whether I like it or not,
I must wait.
Whether a long period or short,
I must wait.
Though I'm betrayed and I know,

I must wait.
For this could be,
My pre-destined fate.

Determination

I could see the deep night sky;
Displaying the beautiful stars;
Though there were many, WAY too many;
I was forced to pick just one.

My aim was to look after my beautiful star;
To give it all that my heart could offer;
Neither the Sun nor the Moon could take it
away;
No, not even Mother Nature.

I was told to be careful when picking this star;
And those words came more like a warning;
I was not to concentrate on the star's brightness;
For its brightness could change in the morning.

I was certain that my star would not fade;
Regardless of the approaching dusk;
No matter what those around me said,
I was determined to fulfil my task.

This task was to Love Endlessly;
Even through the hardest predicaments;
So I did what myself could only do best;
For 'twas the only thing what made sense.

The only way to know if I succeeded;
Is to ask my precious star;
I'm sure I achieved my goals as 'twas said;
There's no one better than I.

Transformation

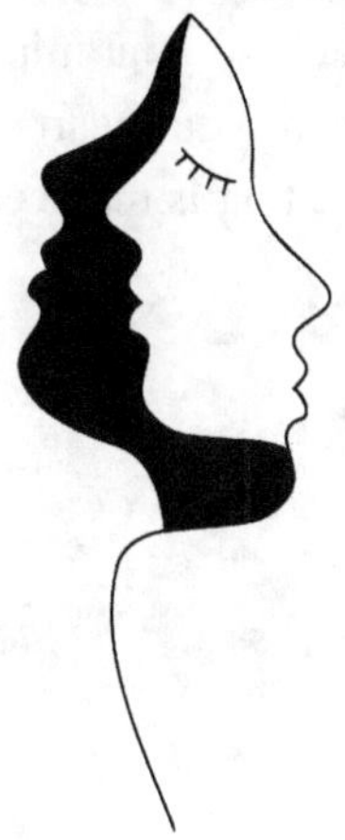

Yes, it makes sense;
Change is inevitable,
A moment of essentiality
That persists to occur.

It is the balance
that we all walk through.
Slowly but surely,
Silently riding the air
Growing, adjusting, transforming.

Change, a blessing designed to be strong
Only for that moment,
The only thing that can comprehend
The brokenness of a fixed soul.

Change remains undermined,
Through the corners of your mind,
and the memories of your heart,
Until it is a course that is made clear.

Violent Love

There's a different kind of violence. You know?
Not the violence with grenades or machine guns,
But the violence of the soul, heart and mind.
The kind of violence where some use Love,
As a bomb to shatter lives.
While others use the same love as a crutch to
hold on to.
Seldom caring for whatever wreckage is left
behind.

Now don't get me wrong, I believe in love,
Or at least the notion of it, it's kinda nice.
But I fell in love, once, twice, too many times.
Each time coming to the realisation that,
People will use you, at every chance they get.
All to satisfy their pleasures.
With little concern about your being.
Such terrible regret.

Now, I'm not trying to put a black cloud,
Over the emotions that we may feel,
The emotions that may surround our lives.
But, at the end of the day, you gotta ask,
What's the point of it all?
'Cause it's all so strange to me, this love.

Because see, I love love,
But love doesn't seem to love me back.

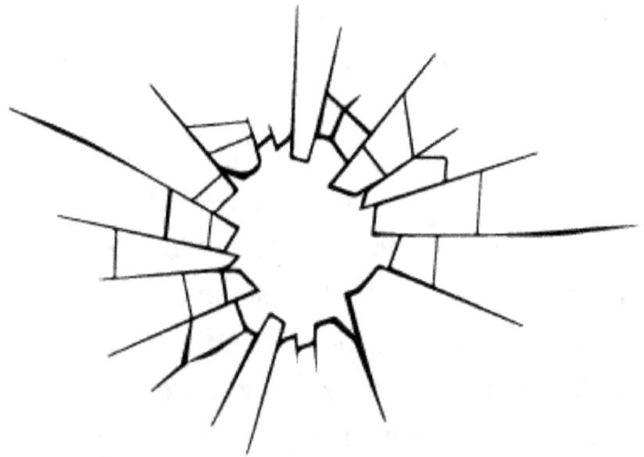

Careful

Careful
They'll make you bitter, they will.
Careful, they played you to their will,
Gathered intel deep in your hearts well,
Having anchored themselves to your soul,
Where your first trust game fell.

Careful
They'll make you bitter they will.
Revenge
Is not a dish best-served cold.
For your soul holds traces of gold,
And if you're careless, you'll give gold out
To them, with each blow that you take,
So hang tight, soon you'll feel awake.

Careful
Like a racket in the silence,
A disturber of peace,
Freedom
Is not as free as they market.
For memories, they work in abundance.
The act of forgetting suggests you never lived,
And we know your life and sanity supercede
Denials of the pain that you once used to bear.

Careful
They took time to use you
and empty out all of your love, but,
Pain
is worse when it settles within,
than when it is given without.
Maybe, with all that wasted time
Your character has been refined.
For perhaps it is the hardships that define who
you really are.

Fearful Love

Well,
You say you don't deserve me,
But Darling when I look in the mirror
And gaze at my tattered soul,
The eyes staring back at me
Know, How far-fetched your observation is.

For I,
I am but a human-machine.
Connected fine, yet harbouring,
Broken parts deep within.
Like the pain of a Clock
Which has no tick or tock

I mean,
I know you mean well.
But as my fears deepen
Further around my heart,
Caution spreads internally,
Like ivy, on the roughened walls.

I don't trust myself
To let another Lover in.
My softened Being is far too weak
To rescue me from another plunge

Into the abyss of sorrows.
So I take leave,

Disappear,
Back into the safety of my silence.
Without haste. See all, Say nothing.
For the burden of Love.
Can weigh a ton,
Stop you in your tracks
Like a Fiend when it has won.

So I do not want it,
Yet, I cannot chase it away.
For my strength has strayed
And my patience has relayed, the agony
That forces my hands to remain static.
Barely able to hold on to my sanity.

For the fear of caring for you,
Leaves me frozen with "desire"
An emotion I banned in times past.
Though my heart aches for you,
I let you seep through my fingers,
Like the sand in our hourglass.

I cannot keep you for your sake,
And you cannot love me for mine.
So to avoid the game of lovers' band,
I shall walk away from you, in a rush;

Not because I have seized to care about you
But it's because I do, that I must dash…

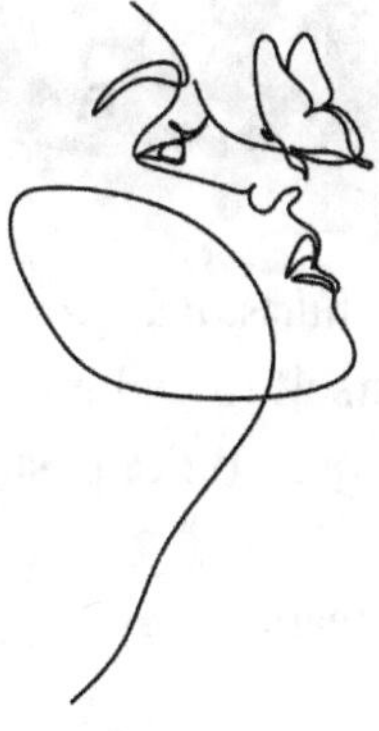

Grief

Feel it. I know it hurts, badly.
Still, permit yourself to feel it.
The heavy emotions you're pushing away.
Feel them.
Do not keep the tears at bay.
Let them flow,
Release them.

The ultimate gift
you can give yourself,
Is honesty in who you are.
Honesty in how you are.
And honesty in what aligns with your soul
For you ought to know,
Your feelings are not a mere game.

New Reality

Yellow feathers
Like the shade of the sun
Warm, fluffy and happy
Are the memories of my mind
          A fondness of who I once was
Yellow feathers
Bright and warm
Is this a feeling of home;
Of you and me as one, as we belong?
          An adventure has indeed begun

Yellow feathers
Look where you are
In the middle of night
You've claimed your stand
          Helping me to reside, like the Sun is to
the Sky

Yellow feathers
New to your sight
Are these buildings
Of what has become
          In a place where longer days now keep
you by and by

Cleansing Rain

Let the rain pour down on me,
Perhaps it can wash away my tears.
Let the rain pour down on me,
I don't want to shed any more tears.

Let the rain pour down on me,
New beginnings are on the horizon.
Let the rain pour down on me,
I'm no longer in the dark the light is on.

Let the rain pour down on me,
Help me forget bad things past.
Let the rain pour down on me,
Allow this new happiness to last.

Because when the rain has finished pouring,
And the warm sun has come out.
And the gentle breeze feels soft on my skin,
I will have a clue, of what life is about.

Madness My Friend

Madness is my friend and insanity is my
companion.
If all the sense of the world was placed at the
edge of a pen,
Then all my miserable dreams would find
themselves lost on a page.

Madness is my friend and insanity is my
companion.
Lose all the lies and find the truth, it is hiding
somewhere, anywhere,
In an unfamiliar place, between me and you and
rage.

Madness is my friend and insanity is my
companion.
If my thoughts flowed the way my heart showed
them to,
Then my eyes could almost see what was ahead
for me and for you.

Madness is my friend and insanity is my
companion.
Not a single thing makes sense, in a world with
no passion.

So, Madness my dear friend, and insanity my
dearest companion,
It is now your time to show off your actions.

I wear yellow

I wear yellow
Not because I'm happy
Or deliriously glad
It's a costume
I pretend I'm not sad

As the hollow days draw nigh
I remember a much younger I
With high hopes and dreams
full to the brim with desire
Never asking why

With my tender heart I aimed
To live the dreams I dreamt
A reality of comforts
Within the years I've spent

Yet here I am
Very much Older
and questionably wiser
Alone in a world full of people

Heart Melodies

Unsung words
Of a song I've written
Time and time again
My heart covered and smitten
In lyrics all so real
Of a world only I feel

Unsung words
Of a song I've written
Where do I fit in?
I'm like a tailor's pin
That weighs down the dresses
When being hemmed in—with linen

Unsung words
Of a song I've written
I know of a culture
That sits within me, I am who I am
And you are who you are
The rest is in-between

Unsung words
Of a song I've written
I mither my soul
To reminisce again

Of the events, birthdays, celebrations
That have long gone

The Unsung words
Of the songs I've written
Have a tone of their own
Desperate to be heard
Deep within my heart
Is where I keep them
But if you hush and listen
You might just hear them

Love Is Not Blind

Don't let them lie to you,
There is nothing blind about love.
It has a cornea and an iris.
It has pupils that freely dilate,
Without giving them a shove.

Come to think of it,
I'm almost certain that it has teeth too.
It can chew you through and through,
With no time taken to hesitate,
Tricking you into thinking you are beloved.

Just Because I Love You

Just because I love you,
Doesn't mean you'll love me back.
I could waver all advances and
Pretend you're all mine,
But in the end, it doesn't mean jack.
See, because you only offer me halves,
Yet I tell myself I have no lack.
But I'm wrong. And it sucks.
Still, I love you, I always have.

Although you were my all,
I was merely your pastime.
My fault. I know. I forced your hand.
Truth be told, I ain't even mad,
Cause I knew exactly the potion,
The notion of what you held in your hand,

Right from the start, I saw your cards.
But every time I attempted to leave,
I'd receive a giant hole in my heart...
So I stayed.

Stuck at a cross between
The fear of being alone,
And not being able to find the right one.
Because the reality was I liked you,
Heck, I'm sure I actually loved you.
I was ready to say "I do"
Trade in loneliness, for the gentle kisses
You placed on my forehead to say g'night.
The way you'd hold me so tight
Each time we hugged... It felt nice.
I was like a child in your arms,
Confident, comfortable, with eyes wide shut.

You didn't even try to hide your play,
And yet still I loved you anyway.
So the truth is I can't blame you,
For never wanting to stay.
Because deep down I knew,
Although I tried to delay,
I was always the one who was going to pay,
The price of forcing love on you,
A love that perhaps made you feel blue.

Let It Be

So long I've clung to you
Hoping that soon enough
You'd find me enough
And worthy of your time
But we can both see
That is not the case

When I'm talking to you
We're arguing and when
We're not talking we're worlds apart
As if two strangers
Meeting for the first time
So I wish to depart

This ship of confusion
And false hope
Has taken enough of our time
Let it be, let it be
Let it be.

Death The Robber

Dear Death,
You disrespectful, selfish,
self-centred, self-serving
pain-inducing,
energy-draining-prick.
You are a good for nothing thief

The people you leave behind
In your wake are not toys.
We feel the shards, that you wedge
Deep inside our hearts,
When you rip our loved ones away from us.
Far away from us, into your nameless abyss,
Painfully reminding us that,
We cannot control you.

Your singular aim is to take up
So. Much. Space. Mocking,
Sniggering at us, knowing
We cannot ignore you.
Knowing, you will NOT
move out of the way.

Dear Death.
What do you have against souls being alive?

Hope

When you have opened a door, any door,
Then you have agreed to gaily dance,
Said yes to opportunity and chance
Accepted the melody of life.

When you have opened a door, any door,
Then you have said good-bye to sorrows
Prepared your Soul for tomorrow,
Eliminated your every strife.

When you have opened a door,
Everyday breathes a new hope,
A new reason to live and feel refreshed,
Ready for the lessons that it strives to bring.

When you have opened a door, any door,
And you see familiar faces,
Be sure to take a moment and rest;
Because, there, there is a place called Home.

The Red Sea

Here, I remain calm.
Never have my eyes
beheld such marvellous beauty.
Untouched, perfect, serene.
With no sound of alarm.

Far beyond man's influence,
The life below the surface keeps on.
I had seen it before,
Inside a TV screen I'm sure .

Yet, nothing could prepare me,
For the wonder that held my gaze,
As I dived below the water,
I was amazed

I found peace,
Perfect blue peace,
Down there.
Yes, there's not much that's red,
Under the Red Sea.

Hate

Once HATE has overwhelmed your mind;
Slowly consuming your body and soul,
Then, it has reached its targeted rationale;
Offending everything within its grasp—

It can no longer stay sheltered, introvert beneath
its veil
For its perseverance is utterly surreal.
It survives on destruction and pandemonium;
Allowing only soreness, agony and hurt to give
it, it's thrill—

Like a very quiet seeker, hunter, predator;
It catches, even the alert, without prior notice,
Contravening and consuming until nothing is
left,
In effect, not even room for weeping—

It has no compassion, nor harmony, nor zeal;
For these are merely strange emotions in its
presence,
Longing to take over, not only your soul;
But patronising and controlling the souls around
you—

Don't smile at it; it is dangerous!
Don't laugh with it; it is dangerous!
Don't talk to it; it is dangerous!
There must be no communication whatsoever
                    Lest it devours you.

Change

My shadow fell into your light
A paradox of this blatant sight
This pain, oh sweet glorious pain
That forces my wings to take flight

I cannot fly, I cannot fly
I've never been shown how
So here I stay, here I'll remain
Won't you tend to me now?

I feel your presence ever so near
Although I stand chained to this fear
Let me hold your hand, please help me stand
Support my feeble stance.

No matter, we're here once again,
For one reason or another
We must move. I guess all is well.
For soon, I shall be with the others.

Climate - Soulmate

We fit, you and I,
Like a glove fits to a hand
A perfect match; a belonging
To a place, to a friend
To a pure heart…

As your presence and my presence clasp
We unite and adjust always,
Keeping close to purpose,
Climbing always, nothing less
Just mysteries…

We suffer no judgements,
For we understand each other
We are who we are
Always advancing up the ladder

You rain on me,
So I hide under the shelter
Of my purple umbrella
Smiling at the raindrops
They remind me of what it feels like;
To listen to my senses…

Hobo

Standing here confused;
On which road to take,
I desire not to run
So here I shall remain.

They say I have no home,
No place where I belong,
Yet home is where my heart is
So home is here with me.

Alone, alone, I walk along.
Solitary through these realms,
These places, that are right or at times are wrong

But, I stand ready to take them on.

Following no footsteps,
But leaving a trail to be seen.
A trail of hope, to maybe return to,
The places where I have been.

On and on, unaccompanied I stay
Engrossed in concerns of my own.
Prepared to indulge in these new places,
Of the shadowy sights that my eyes have drawn.

Walking through fresh roads alone,
Freedom is here with me, so I carry myself
along.
Hand in hand, my soul and I glide,
Pensive, and at times, ready to hide.

They say I have no home,
No place where I belong.
But home is where my heart is,
So, home is here with me.